W9-AUI-631

Smelling

CHELSEA CLUBHOUSE

An Imprint of Chelsea House Publishers

A Haights Cross Communications Company

Philadelphia

Kimberley Jane Pryor

For Nick, Ashley and Thomas

Chelsea Clubhouse
1974 Sproul Road, Suite 400
Broomall, PA 19008-0914

The Chelsea House world wide web address is www.chelseahouse.com

Library of Congress Cataloging-in-Publication Data

Pryor, Kimberley Jane.
    Smelling / Kimberley Jane Pryor.
    p. cm. — (The senses)

    Includes index.
    Contents: Your senses — Your nose — Smelling — A message to your brain — All kinds of smells — Smelling danger — Smell and taste — Smell and memory — Protecting your nose — Using all your senses.

    ISBN 0-7910-7556-7
    1. Smell—Juvenile literature. [1. Smell. 2. Nose. 3. Senses and sensation.] I. Title. II. Series.
    QP458.P79 2004
    612.8'6—dc21

                                                                            2003001175

First published in 2003 by
MACMILLAN EDUCATION AUSTRALIA PTY LTD
627 Chapel Street, South Yarra, Australia, 3141

Associated companies and representatives throughout the world.

Copyright © Kimberley Jane Pryor 2003

Page layout by Raul Diche
Illustrations by Alan Laver, Shelly Communications
Photo research by Legend Images

Printed in China

Acknowledgements
Cover photograph: girl smelling flowers, courtesy of Getty Images/Taxi.

Artville, p. 14 (top left); Coo-ee Picture Library, p. 14 (top right); Corbis Digital Stock, p. 14 (center left); Digital Vision, p. 7; The DW Stock Picture Library, p. 15; Getty Images/Image Bank, p. 26; Getty Images/Stone, p. 8; Getty Images/Taxi, pp. 1, 4, 10, 12, 13, 28; Great Southern Stock, pp. 5, 16, 25; Nick Milton, pp. 6, 23, 27, 29; Photodisc, pp. 14 (bottom left and right, center right), 17, 18, 21, 22; Photolibrary.com, p. 20;
Terry Oakley/The Picture Source, p. 19.

While every care has been taken to trace and acknowledge copyright, the publisher tenders their apologies for any accidental infringement where copyright has proved untraceable. Where the attempt has been unsuccessful, the publisher welcomes information that would redress the situation.

Please note
At the time of printing, the Internet addresses appearing in this book were correct. Owing to the dynamic nature of the Internet, however, we cannot guarantee that all these addresses will remain correct.

Contents

Your Senses

You have five senses to help you learn about the world. They are smell, sight, hearing, taste, and touch.

You smell flowers with your nose.

Smelling

You smell by breathing in or sniffing air through your nose. Your sense of smell tells you about the odors, or smells, in your surroundings and warns you of danger.

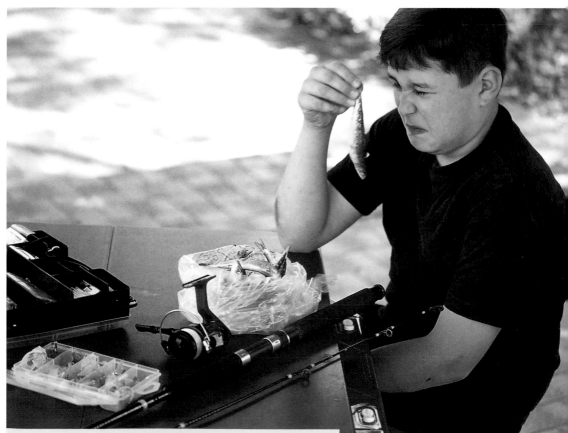

Your nose tells you if something smells bad.

Your Nose

Noses come in different shapes and sizes. They can be big or small, flat or pointed, straight or crooked.

Your nose has two openings called nostrils, which are separated by a wall called the septum. You breathe air in and out through your nostrils.

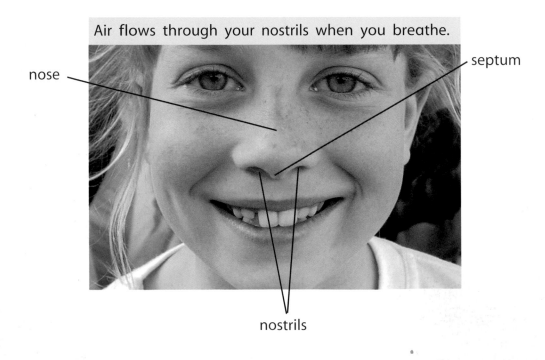

Air flows through your nostrils when you breathe.

nose

septum

nostrils

A soft, thin **mucous membrane** lines the inside of your nose. This layer of **tissue** makes a wet, slimy liquid called mucus. The mucous membrane also has tiny hairs called **cilia**. The mucus and cilia trap dust and germs so you do not breathe them into your lungs.

Your nose filters dust out of the air you breathe in.

Smelling

Odors come from tiny gas **molecules** that float in the air. The gas molecules are released by people, animals, plants, foods, and other objects around you.

There are many odors in a supermarket.

When you breathe in, air and gas molecules travel through each nostril and into an area called the nasal cavity. Some of the gas molecules reach **olfactory nerve cells** at the top of the nasal cavity.

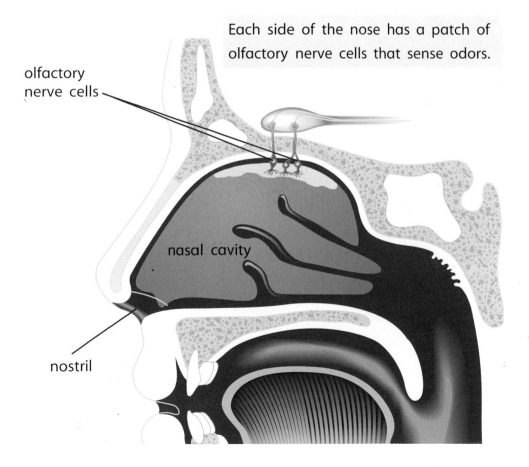

Each side of the nose has a patch of olfactory nerve cells that sense odors.

olfactory nerve cells

nasal cavity

nostril

The gas molecules **dissolve** in the mucus covering the olfactory nerve cells. Each cell has cilia covered with tiny **receptors** that sense what type of odor is present.

Odors from food travel through the air and into your nose.

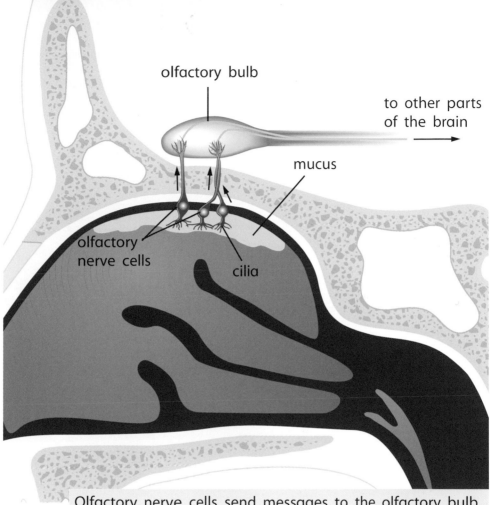

olfactory bulb

to other parts of the brain

mucus

olfactory nerve cells

cilia

Olfactory nerve cells send messages to the olfactory bulb.

The olfactory nerve cells send signals to a part of the brain called the **olfactory bulb**. From there, signals are sent to other parts of the brain.

A Message to Your Brain

When the olfactory bulb sends out a message, your brain decides what the odor is and whether you should do something about it.

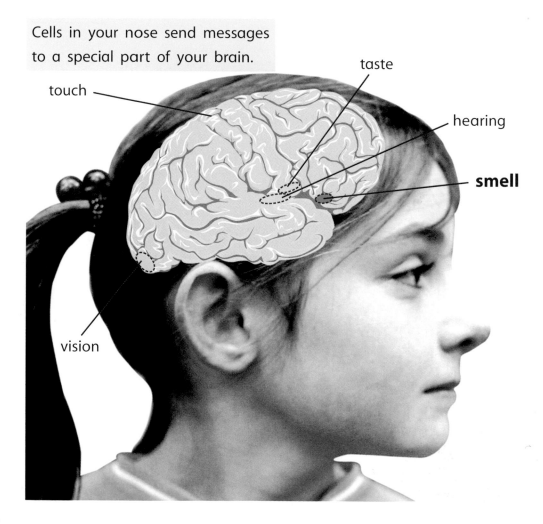

Cells in your nose send messages to a special part of your brain.

touch

taste

hearing

smell

vision

When you smell a hot dog, your olfactory nerve cells send a message to your brain. Then your brain sends a message to your mouth to tell it to get ready to eat.

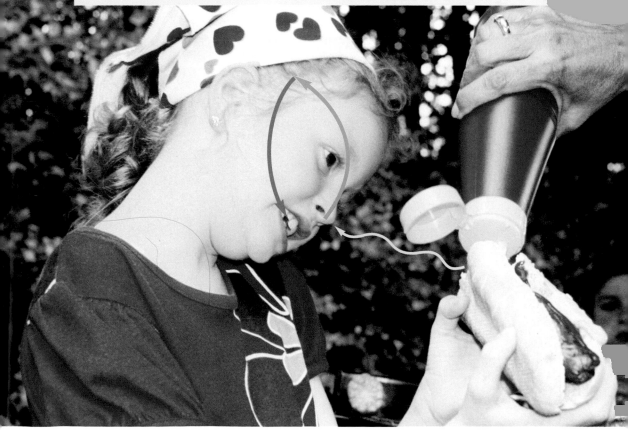

Some odors send a signal to your brain to get you ready to eat.

Minty smells

Some smells are minty. Candy canes have a peppermint smell. Your toothpaste probably has a minty odor to make your breath smell fresh and clean.

Some toothpastes have a minty odor.

Sharp or spicy smells

Onions, cloves, and cinnamon give off sharp or spicy odors. Some of these odors can make your eyes water, especially if you breathe them in through your nose. Spices add flavor to your food.

Onion has a sharp smell.

Sweet smells

Foods that smell sweet often contain sugar. Fruits such as strawberries and bananas have a sweet odor. So does chocolate!

Ripe fruit smells sweet.

Fresh smells

Things that are new and clean smell fresh. The air outside smells fresh after it rains. Your favorite shirt has a fresh odor after it has been washed and dried. You smell fresh, too, after a bath!

Washed and dried towels smell fresh.

19

Smelling Danger

Your sense of smell helps warn you of danger. When you smell smoke, a signal goes to your brain to tell you to move away from a fire.

The strong smell of smoke tells you to move away.

When you smell rotting garbage in a dump, your brain tells you the dump is dangerous.

Garbage has a bad odor.

Your sense of smell also tells you when food is rotten and not safe to eat. Have you ever smelled sour milk, moldy bread, or old fish?

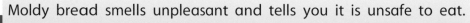
Moldy bread smells unpleasant and tells you it is unsafe to eat.

Try this!

Ask a parent or teacher for help.

How sensitive is your nose?

⭐ Collect different foods, such as peppermints, garlic, bananas, oranges, peanut butter, and chocolate. Keep them hidden.

⭐ Ask a friend to close his or her eyes and to smell each food one at a time.

⭐ Ask, "Do you know this smell?"

⭐ Can your friend tell what each food is by its smell?

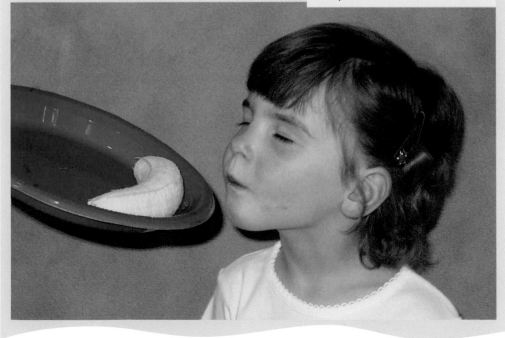

Do you know this smell?

23

Smell and Taste

Your sense of smell also helps you taste. When you eat, odors float from the food and from the back of your mouth into your nose. Your sense of smell and your sense of taste work together to tell you the flavor of food.

You sense the flavor of food from both its smell and taste.

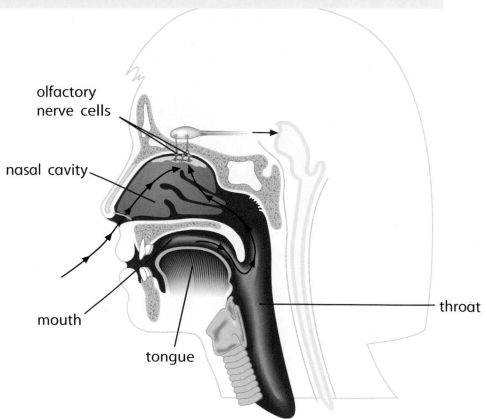

olfactory
nerve cells

nasal cavity

mouth

tongue

throat

When you have a cold, your food seems to lose its taste.

Remember the last time you were sick with a cold? You probably could not smell very well, and you probably could not taste much either. This happened because the thick mucus in your nose stopped the food odors from reaching your olfactory nerve cells.

Smell and Memory

Messages from your nose go to parts of your brain that store feelings and memories. This is why certain odors remind you of people or places.

The smell of popcorn may remind you of a trip to the movies.

Try this!

Ask a parent or teacher for help.

Make memory jars

⭐ Put liquids such as baby lotion, liquid soap, bubble bath, and sunscreen lotion into separate jars.

⭐ Sniff each jar until a smell brings back a memory.

⭐ In a notebook, write down the name of the odor and the memory it brings to mind.

You will see how your sense of smell and your memory are connected.

The smell of bubble bath may remind you of playing in the bath.

Protecting Your Nose

Your sense of smell is important and helps you enjoy life. So, protect your nose to keep it healthy!

- ⊗ Never put food or objects into your nose.
- ⊗ See a doctor if the mucus in your nose turns yellow or green.
- ⊗ Cover your nose when the air is dusty, smoky, or **polluted**.

Some workers wear masks to keep dust out of their noses.

It is important to be careful when you smell something new, just in case it is dangerous.

What to do

⭐ Hold the open container about six inches (15 centimeters) away from your face.

⭐ Wave your hand over the opening of the container to move the smell toward your nose.

Use the "safety sniff" when you smell something unknown.

Using All Your Senses

You need your senses to smell, see, hear, taste, and touch things. The best way to learn about the world around you is to use all your senses.

Did You Know?
You can probably smell better than many of the adults you know. As people grow older, their sense of smell gets worse.

Did You Know?
People who cannot smell have a condition called anosmia.

Did You Know?
Many animals have a better sense of smell than humans. Saint Bernard dogs use their keen sense of smell to find people who are buried under the snow.

Glossary

cilia	tiny, hair-like structures attached to cells in certain parts of the body
dissolve	to mix something in a liquid so that it becomes part of the liquid
molecules	the tiniest forms of matter
mucous membrane	a thin tissue that covers the inside of the nose and produces a liquid called mucus
olfactory bulb	the part of the brain above the nasal cavity that receives messages from the olfactory nerve cells and sends messages on to other parts of the brain
olfactory nerve cells	specialized cells located at the top of the nasal cavity; each cell has receptors that identify odors.
polluted	dirty or unhealthy
receptors	the nerve cells at the end of the sensory nerves which receive messages and send signals along the nerve to the brain
tissue	a group of cells that forms a part of a plant, or an animal's or a person's body, such as a heart or muscle

Index

Web Sites

You can go to these web sites to learn more about the sense of smell:

http://www.kidshealth.org/kid/body/nose_SW.html

http://yucky.kids.discovery.com/noflash/body/pg000150.html

http://whyfiles.larc.nasa.gov/text/kids/Problem_Board/problems/stink/smell2b.html